The Kids' Career Library™

A Day in the Life of a
Teacher

Mary Bowman-Kruhm

The Rosen Publishing Group's

PowerKids Press™
New York

Thanks to Carol Young, principal, and to David Titus, teacher, Hillcrest Elementary School, Frederick County (MD) Public Schools, for their cooperation and help.

Published in 1999 by The Rosen Publishing Group, Inc.
29 East 21st Street, New York, NY   10010

First Edition

Book Design: Erin McKenna

Photo Illustrations: All photos by Ethan Zindler.

Bowman-Kruhm, Mary.
     A day in the life of a teacher / by Mary Bowman-Kruhm.
          p.   cm. — (The kids' career library)
     Includes index.
     Summary: Explores a typical day in the work of a third-grade teacher, describing his activities in the classroom, lunchroom, and teachers' meeting.
     ISBN 0-8239-5295-9
     1. Elementary school teachers—Juvenile literature. 2. Teaching—Vocational guidance—Juvenile literature. [1. Teachers. 2. Occupations.] I. Title. II. Series.
LB1776.B59   1998
372.11—DC21

                                                                              98-5093
                                                                                 CIP
                                                                                  AC

Manufactured in the United States of America

Contents

Starting the Day

At 8:00 in the morning, Mr. Titus begins his day as a teacher. He writes the **objectives** (ub-JEK-tivz) for his third-grade class on the board before the class arrives. Mr. Titus always thinks about what he's going to do before each day begins. "Kids learn more if they know what I expect them to do each day," he says.

◄ Writing the class objectives on the board helps Mr. Titus as well as the class to plan their day.

"Good Morning!"

Mr. Titus greets the students as they enter the classroom. He says "Good morning! How are you?" to every student. After the students put away their backpacks and coats, they write in their **journals** (JER-nuhlz). Some students don't want anyone to see what they write. That's okay. Others like to share what they have written with each other and with Mr. Titus.

Then, the school TV **newscast** (NEWZ-kast) tells everyone to stand for the Pledge of Allegiance and gives the news of the day.

The students like that Mr. Titus greets them ▶ each morning before the day begins.

Calendar Time

Each morning, Mr. Titus points to the calendar. "Look at the calendar," he says to the class. "Here's a problem to solve: What **pattern** (PA-tern) of shapes and colors do you notice when you look at the calendar? Thinking about what you see is important."

The students notice that the shapes on the calendar make **diagonal** (dy-AG-nul) patterns. They write down this answer.

"That's right! Good job!" says Mr. Titus.

◀ The calendar in Mr. Titus's classroom helps the students learn not only about dates but about shapes, patterns, and colors.

A Quiz!

Next Mr. Titus and the class play a game to review math problems. Then he tells the class to get ready for a math quiz, or short test. Even though they wrote "Quiz" in their notebooks yesterday, the students groan. Mr. Titus laughs and passes out the quiz papers. "When you're done, we'll go outside for recess," he says. When the students hear the word recess, they all quickly get to work.

Sometimes Mr. Titus uses flash cards in class ▶ to help his students with their math skills.

Time to Read

After recess, it's time for **language arts** (LANG-wij ARTZ). Today, the students read a story about ocean animals. Mr. Titus asks them questions about the story to help them understand what they have read. He tries to find stories that fit with the students' work in social studies and science.

Then, the students are able to read books that interest them during free reading. "If I let the kids choose what they want to read, then they'll read more," he says. Mr. Titus reads his own book too. Everyone enjoys reading!

◀ If a student has a hard time with part of his book, Mr. Titus will help him.

A Problem at Lunch

At lunch, a boy and a girl start to argue. Mr. Titus pulls them aside. He talks with each of them about how they can solve their problem. The three of them talk about the problem. At last the boy and girl shake hands and smile at each other.

"I want my students to grow up to be good and smart grown-ups," Mr. Titus says. "If I can do something every day to make my students feel good about themselves, I've done my job."

Being a teacher is about more than just teaching lessons. ▶ It's also about showing kids how to act with each other.

Meeting with Other Teachers

While the students go to their art and music classes, Mr. Titus talks with other third-grade teachers. The teachers are planning a field trip for the entire third grade. Because the trip will take a lot of work, each teacher decides to do one job for the trip. One teacher will help with the busses. Another will pass out permission slips. All of the teachers work together. After the meeting, Mr. Titus rushes back to his classroom. Soon, his students will return, and he still has to call two parents and make copies of **materials** (muh-TEER-ee-uhlz) for science. Hurry Mr. Titus!

◀ All the third-grade teachers will share the work as they prepare for the field trip.

Science Is Like Baseball

Near the end of the day the class studies science. Mr. Titus shows the students how to do an **experiment** (ek-SPEHR-ih-mint). Then all of the students do the experiment.

"Learning science is like being on a baseball team. Kids who sit on the bench during the whole game won't learn because they're not playing," he tells them. In science, Mr. Titus wants everyone to play in the game. They learn science by doing the experiment.

Doing an experiment helps the students to better understand the science lesson. ▶

The End of the Day

After their science experiment, the students clean up and get ready to go home. Before they leave, Mr. Titus asks them: "What did we learn today?" The students talk about language arts and science and what they read that day.

As they walk out the door, Mr. Titus tells each student, "Have a nice night!" It has been a busy day. He is tired. But Mr. Titus is happy knowing the students will have a lot to say when their parents ask them what they did in school today.

◀ Mr. Titus likes to talk with his students. He hopes his students feel comfortable talking with him too.

More to Do

Mr. Titus's day isn't over yet. He must put away books and plan for tomorrow. He must prepare materials. He must grade quizzes and decide if each student is ready to move ahead or needs to review a subject again. He also thinks about how he can help students who are having a hard time outside of school.

"Teaching is not just about book learning," Mr. Titus says. "I became a teacher to help my students as well as teach them." Mr. Titus is a good teacher—he does both of these things.

Glossary

diagonal (dy-AG-nul) A straight line that cuts across in a slanting direction.

experiment (ek-SPEHR-ih-mint) A test to show how something works.

journal (JER-nuhl) A notebook in which students write their thoughts.

language arts (LANG-wij ARTZ) The skills of reading, writing, listening, and speaking.

materials (muh-TEER-ee-uhlz) Papers and supplies that a teacher uses in class.

newscast (NEWZ-kast) Information given by television or radio.

objective (ub-JEK-tiv) The thing a teacher wants students to learn that day.

pattern (PA-tern) A design that is repeated again and again.

Index